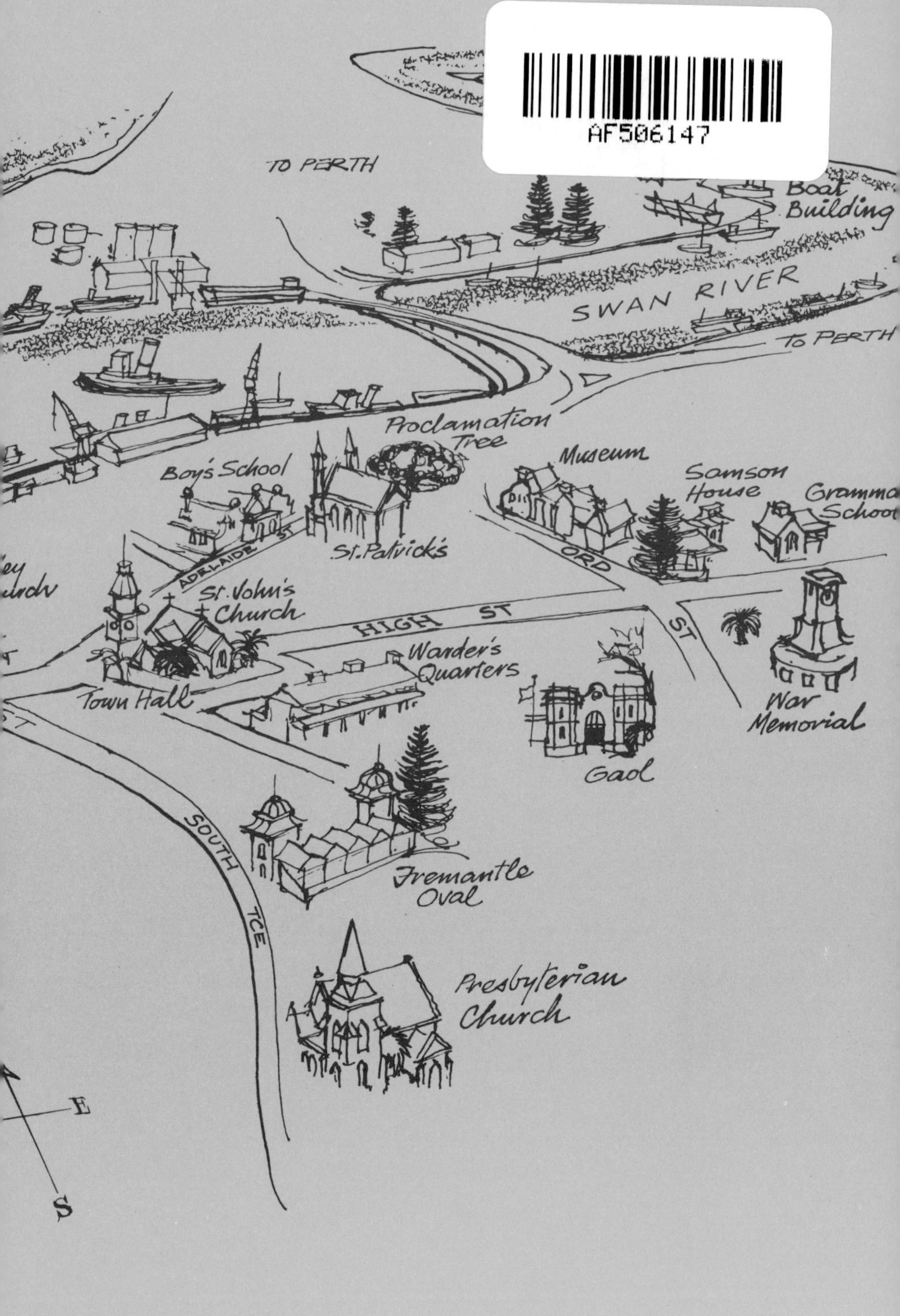

TO PERTH
SWAN RIVER
TO PERTH
Boat Building
Proclamation Tree
Boy's School
Museum
Samson House
Gramma School
St. Patrick's
ADELAIDE
ORD
St. John's Church
HIGH ST
ST
War Memorial
Town Hall
Warder's Quarters
Gaol
SOUTH TCE
Fremantle Oval
Presbyterian Church
E
S

FREMANTLE SKETCHBOOK

Text by
KIRWAN WARD

Drawings by
BRUCE WROTH

RIGBY

RIGBY PUBLISHERS LIMITED • ADELAIDE
SYDNEY • MELBOURNE • BRISBANE • PERTH
NEW YORK • LONDON • AUCKLAND

First published 1974
Reprinted 1976
Revised edition published 1981
Copyright © Bruce Wroth and Kirwan Ward 1974
ISBN 0 85179 691 5
All rights reserved
Wholly designed and set up in Australia
Printed in Hong Kong

CONTENTS

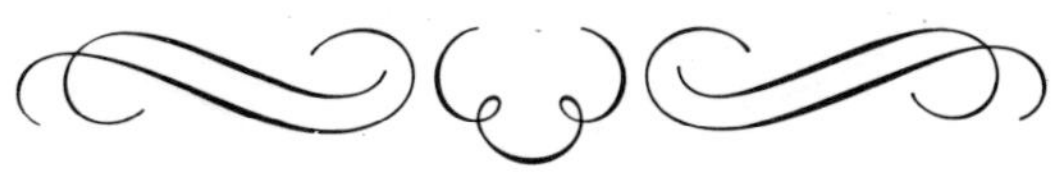

ROUND HOUSE

"The weather being unsettled and boisterous," wrote Captain Charles Fremantle, from his cabin in the Royal Navy frigate H.M.S. *Challenger*, "it was not until the second day of May that I could land at the Swan River, distant 9½ miles from Cockburn Sound; on that day formal possession was taken of the whole of the west coast of New Holland in the name of His Britannic Majesty, and the Union Jack was hoisted at the south head of the river."

The spot where that historic flag flapped in the boisterous weather was almost certainly Arthur Head (later known as Gaol Hill), the south head of the present Fremantle harbour. It was there that Western Australia's oldest surviving building, the Round House, was built two years later, to the design of the colony's first civil engineer, Henry Reveley.

At first, the Round House was used as a gaol for minor offenders (serious criminals were transported to Tasmania). Later, it became a police station and lockup. The tunnel through the limestone cliffs below, connecting High Street with what was then the only landing jetty, was cut through in 1837.

Although convicts did not arrive in Western Australia until 1850, and then only at the urgent request of settlers who desperately needed manual labourers, crime and punishment inevitably intrude upon its early history. Stocks, which were soon set up outside the Round House, stood there until 1849. The colony's first execution took place on a gallows erected ten yards north of the entrance. An eighteen-year-old youth from England's Parkhurst reformatory, who had murdered his employer's son at Dandalup, was hanged there, and his body was suspended in chains.

TOWN HALL

It is best to start a tour of Fremantle where Fremantle itself started, on the windy headland called Arthur Head, with the Indian Ocean slapping eternally against the shoreline behind it. Logically, then, the tour should continue down High Street—for High Street marches away from that landing spot straight as a garrison ramrod, all the way to its eastern end at the Town Hall.

Probably few Australian cities have so large and compact a remaining area of their first substantial buildings as Fremantle. A modern visitor sees, and senses, history in every ornate façade of the old town, in the elaborate balconies and balustrades, in the suddenly-discovered scrollwork above a colonial doorway.

By 1884, Melbourne architects Grainger and D'Ebro had submitted plans for an ambitiously elegant town hall to cost £15,000, a sum perilously close to ten years' total council revenue. On 10 September 1885 Governor Broome laid the foundation stone. The Town Hall clock, supplied by a local watchmaker named W. Hooper, cost £748 10s. Its chimes were described as "Cambridge chimes" similar to those in a Liverpool clock-tower.

The day after its opening, on 22 June 1887, the Town Hall staged a children's ball to celebrate Queen Victoria's jubilee. The licensee of the nearby National Hotel tried to push his way past the acting doorman, Councillor Snook. He was refused admission. Incensed, the publican went back to his hotel, returned with a loaded pistol and shot the councillor, who died a few days later. The hotelier was convicted of wilful murder, and in spite of vigorous petitions for reprieve, he was hanged at Perth gaol on 18 November 1887. In suffering this fate he made his own morbid contribution to Western Australian history, for he was the last person to be executed within the precincts of Perth gaol.

ST JOHN'S CHURCH, KINGS SQUARE

Probably not all Western Australians would know instantly where Kings Square is, for the name derives directly from the old colony. In fact it was, and to some extent still is, the true heart of the city. Bounded by Queen, Adelaide, Newman, and William streets, it encloses two of Fremantle's most historically significant buildings—the Town Hall and St John's Church.

In an 1848 census, 436 of Fremantle's 503 inhabitants gave their religion as Church of England, so perhaps it isn't surprising that this denomination should have established a

church site at the very centre of the settlement as early as 1843.

The present St John's (designed by W. Smith of London) was not opened until 1882. The half of Kings Square on which it stands still belongs to the Anglican Church, and the history-conscious Fremantle City Council has good reason to hope that, with the goodwill of church authorities, it will be possible to preserve the whole square as an entity.

Given wise planning now, this opportunity to preserve entire areas of the old town may well make Fremantle unique. In recent years the Fremantle City Council, by diverting High Street, has already done much to restore the original concept of Kings Square.

Pioneer settlers, whose tastes were so heavily influenced by their British background, would be delighted to see that the grey stone walls and the Welsh slate roof of St John's have mellowed as graciously as a Cotswold village.

GOVERNMENT STORES, CLIFF STREET

Even though so much of the old town is so well preserved, it is difficult to imagine some aspects of Fremantle as it was before the rocky bar was blasted from the mouth of the Swan River, and the inner harbour opened to shipping. C. Y. O'Connor's plan was not implemented until May 1897 when the 2,062-ton s.s. *Sultan*, from Singapore, cleared the partially-excavated bar and slipped into the river.

Harbour work had been going on since 1892, but before this, those arriving at the colony would disembark at a small jetty outside the river mouth, in a tiny bay below Arthur Head. From there they would make their way to High Street by way of the Esplanade and Cliff Street.

Much early history in stone is left all along Cliff Street, though already at least one old building has been lost. The colonial atmosphere haunts this fascinating end of the city as persistently as a friendly ghost.

It is an atmosphere that daily becomes more precious as history elsewhere is ruthlessly squandered. Of all the buildings in Cliff Street, the most architecturally significant is the old Georgian-style Government Store building, erected in 1852 as a commissariat store and office for the Comptroller-General of Convicts.

OLD CUSTOM HOUSE

Again and again, any writer compiling any sort of history of Fremantle, or indeed of the entire Swan River colony, comes back to Cliff Street. It may very well be the most historically significant street in all of Western Australia.

At the street's southernmost end, just before it meets Marine Terrace, is a small, faded, single-storey building, stained with the dust of colonial history. It is set back slightly from today's pavement, with a few of the original imported Yorkshire flagstones at its doorway. This is the old Custom House, built in 1853.

John K. Ewers, in his massively researched *Western Gateway*, notes the suggestion put forward by preservationists that this little building, together with the nearby Government Commissariat and the remaining part of the original Lionel Samson home, might be restored as a complete colonial complex. This could perhaps be used as an old-time market place. It is an imaginative idea, and one that, if followed up, could surely pay off as a tourist attraction.

OLD CUSTOM HOUSE

Built in 1853 as a Military Commissary
Was used as a Custom House until 1903
One of Fremantles oldest buildings.

FREMANTLE CITY COUNCIL
W.A. HISTORICAL SOCIETY
1963

SAMSON BUILDING, CLIFF STREET

The name Samson has been synonymous with Fremantle ever since the founder of this pioneer Western Australian family arrived at the mouth of the Swan River, in the sailing ship *Calista*, in August 1829.

When the first sale of town lots was held only a month later, Lionel Samson acquired Lots 27 and 28. These lots are still owned by a member of the Samson family. Lionel Samson was granted a spirit-merchant's licence, which is in force today, still under the name of Lionel Samson and Son. It is believed to be the oldest continuous licence of this kind in Australia. He built his home here in Cliff Street as part of his business premises. Only half of the old house now remains (it is used as a bond store). The other half was demolished when the adjoining warehouse was rebuilt after a fire in 1898.

There is scarcely any account of early Fremantle activity that doesn't mention the Samsons. When the colony's first horse race was held on South Beach in October 1833, Lionel Samson entered a black mare with a name that would scarcely be appreciated by a modern race-caller. She was called More In Sorrow Than In Anger.

Lionel Samson Building

COURT HOUSE

What we now know as the Old Court House—at the corner of Marine Terrace and Mouat Street—was for a long time called the New Court House, for the building we see today was, in fact, Fremantle's second law-court.

The original was a small building at Arthur Head, alongside the Round House tunnel. This served the colony until the mid-1880s when today's impressive building was erected. In spite of its eminently "court house" appearance, this building was originally intended for, and used mainly as, a police station, even though local courts sat there. Beneath the floors, the outlines of old basement cells can still be seen.

Nineteeth century architects believed in solidity, and the walls of the Court House are two feet thick. Until recently, when repairs were carried out, the roofing was all of lead.

From about 1900 onwards, as Fremantle outgrew the Court House, the place was used for various purposes. It was first tenanted by the Water Supply Department, then in the early 1920s it became a reception centre for migrants. As recently as the 1950s it was a home for alcoholics.

The Court House is within the area of the possible "colonial complex," and the Fremantle Council has notified the State government of its long-term interest in the building.

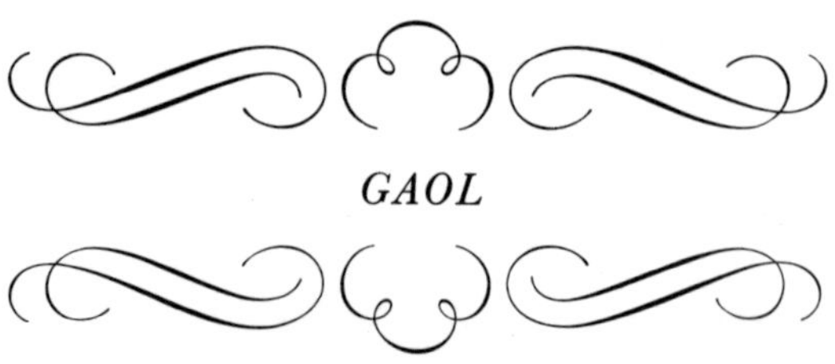

GAOL

Western Australia became a penal settlement only at the request of the settlers who, through their governor, petitioned Her Majesty's Government in Westminster for a desperately needed work force. On 1 June 1850, the first batch of seventy-five convicts, hand-picked for the mildness of their crimes and for their suitability as workmen, arrived at Fremantle in the *Scindian*.

These men, and those that followed them, eventually built their own gaol (1851–59) on a hill above the town. The Governor of Western Australia had previously rejected the proposal by Comptroller-General Henderson that this establishment should be sited on Mount Eliza, above Perth Water.

The original walls and buildings of Fremantle gaol were made from local stone, quarried by convicts. The timber was floated from Woodman's Point, and hauled along the beach by horses.

Modern plans will eventually phase out this gaol, which houses by far the state's largest concentration of prisoners.

The last execution to take place there was that of the multiple-murderer Eric Edgar Cooke, who was hanged on 26 October 1964. The gallows have since been dismantled, and are to be turned over to the Western Australian Historic Society.

The gaol, when vacant, will probably be preserved as an historic monument. The main gateway and the prison chapel, at least, are generally regarded as being worthy of preservation.

WARDERS' QUARTERS

Western Australia's earliest settlers were determined that
the state should never become a penal colony. Twenty years
after the first group of settlers arrived on the *Parmelia*, it was

suggested that the state's crucial man-power shortage should be solved by importing convicts from the United Kingdom. The idea caused bitter divisions in public opinion.

However the *Scindian*, which brought the colony's first batch of prisoners in 1850, also brought fifty-four military pensioners as guards, and with them their families. The gain to the little colony was ninety-seven free citizens.

Not much more than a year later, cottages were built to accommodate these new settlers. These cottages can still be seen in Henderson Street.

HOTELS

Like all seaports, Fremantle has always had at least its fair share of pubs. In the formative years of the 1880s, fastidious visitors left on record disparaging remarks about the proliferation of "grog shops" in the colony. However, there were only four licensed hotels in Fremantle in 1830: the Stirling Arms, the Collins Hotel, the South Sea Hall Public House, and the George IV Public House. By 1843 there were also the Waterman's Arms, the Stag's Head, the Union Hotel, the Albion, and the Crown and Thistle.

Much later, the port had another pub, with the delightful name of His Lordship's Larder. It is surely a pity that some of these old names have disappeared in favour of more commonplace, less colourful nomenclature.

Among the more picturesque survivors of a more picturesque age is the Cleopatra Hotel, in High Street, which was named after a sailing ship of the 1880s. I have been unable to discover exactly when the Cleopatra Hotel was built, but it was certainly in business in 1895, for salvage from the mail steamer *Orizaba* was auctioned here in that year. The *Orizaba* was wrecked on a reef west of Garden Island on 16 February 1895.

In those days, long before the introduction of any kind of cooling systems, the shady trees of the Cleopatra's garden were an attraction that used to be advertised in much the same way as today's hotels advertise air-conditioning.

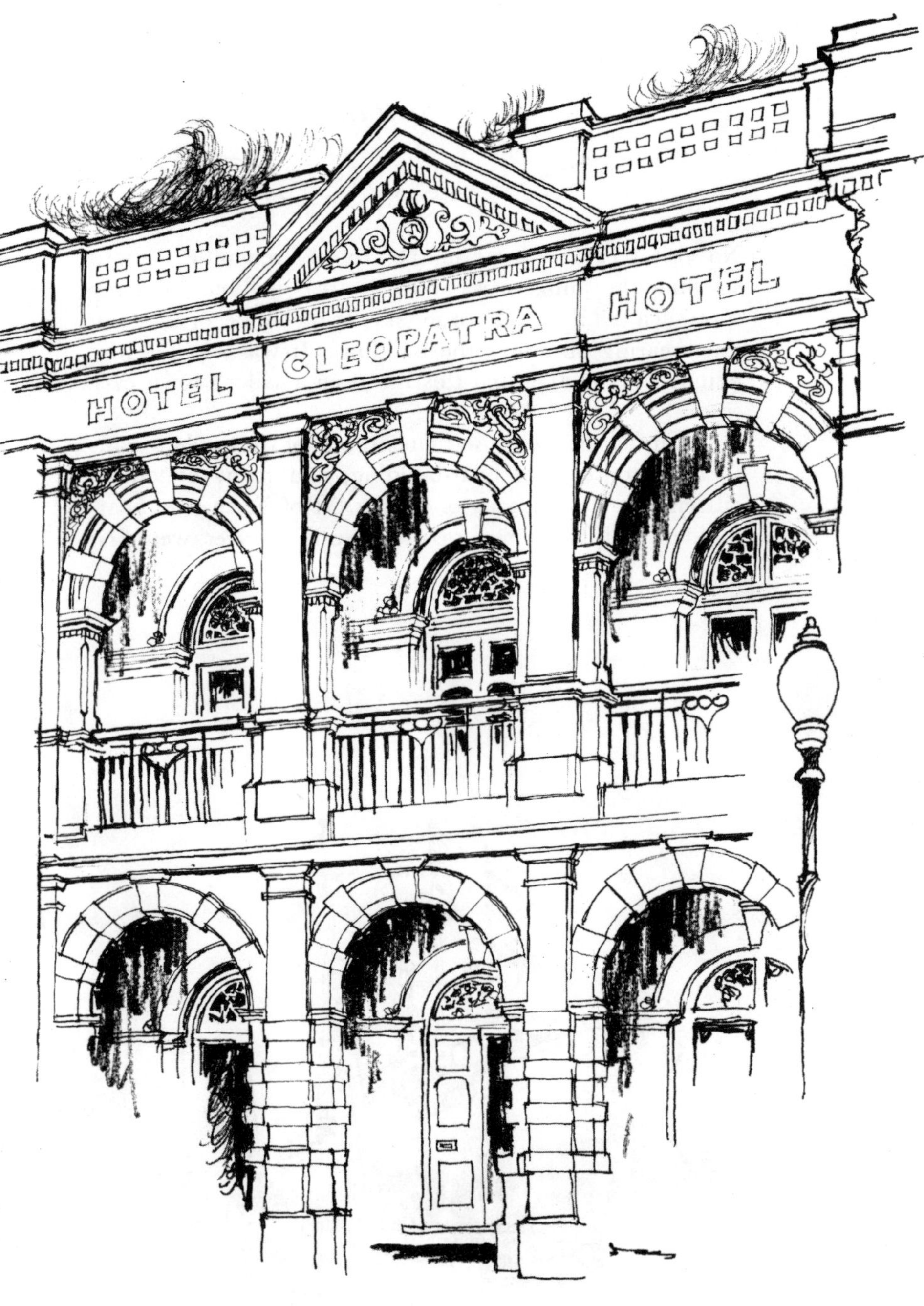

HOTEL
CLEOPATRA HOTEL

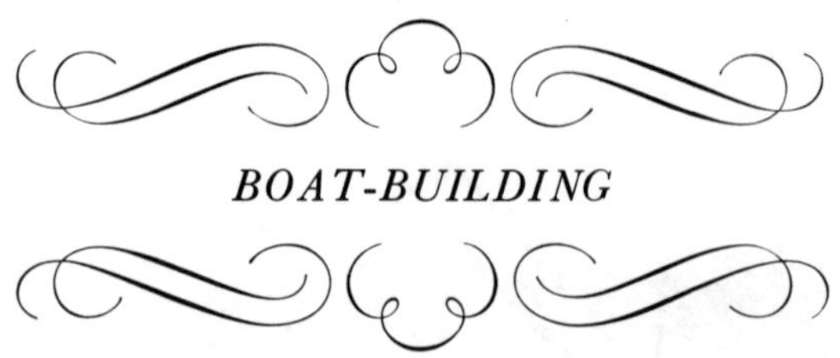

BOAT-BUILDING

No visitor can walk far in the city of Fremantle without smelling the pungent scent of the sea, without suddenly spotting a tall mast against the sky, or the funnel of an ocean liner rearing up above the buildings. It was a sailor who founded Fremantle, and this has been a sailor's town ever since.

Naturally, in such a settlement, one of the earliest crafts to be practised was boat-building, and many of today's citizens are descendants of a long list of Fremantle boat-builders. Shipyards, now predominantly up-river, were first

established at South Beach, where whalers, pearling-luggers, barges, and sailing-ships of all types were built.

The main Perth-Fremantle link was the Swan River, on which sandalwood from York, Toodyay, and Williams would be lightered to Fremantle, for export to Mauritius and Singapore.

One of the first of the pioneer boat-builders and ship-wrights was Thomas W. Mews, who arrived at Fremantle in the *Rockingham*. He is known to have started his trade in Fremantle as early as 1830, less than a year after the foundation of the colony, and he built the first Swan River steamer, the *Speculator*. His sons became well-known for the building of yachts, schooners, and fishing-boats.

Thomas Mews brought his skills from the United Kingdom to the new colony, and Fremantle has always had at least one boat-builder named Mews ever since.

FREMANTLE BOYS' SCHOOL

Though formal education seems to have come slowly to the colony, there is evidence that its wise forefathers were thinking of it right from the start. In 1834 Fremantle, with other settlements, was allotted a sum of fifty pounds for educational purposes, by Governor Sir James Stirling. By

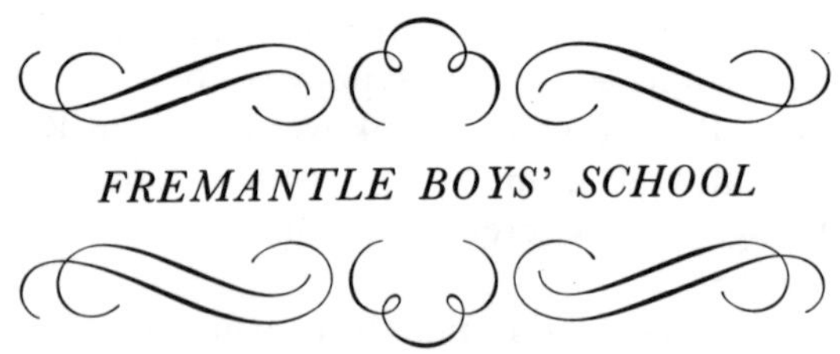

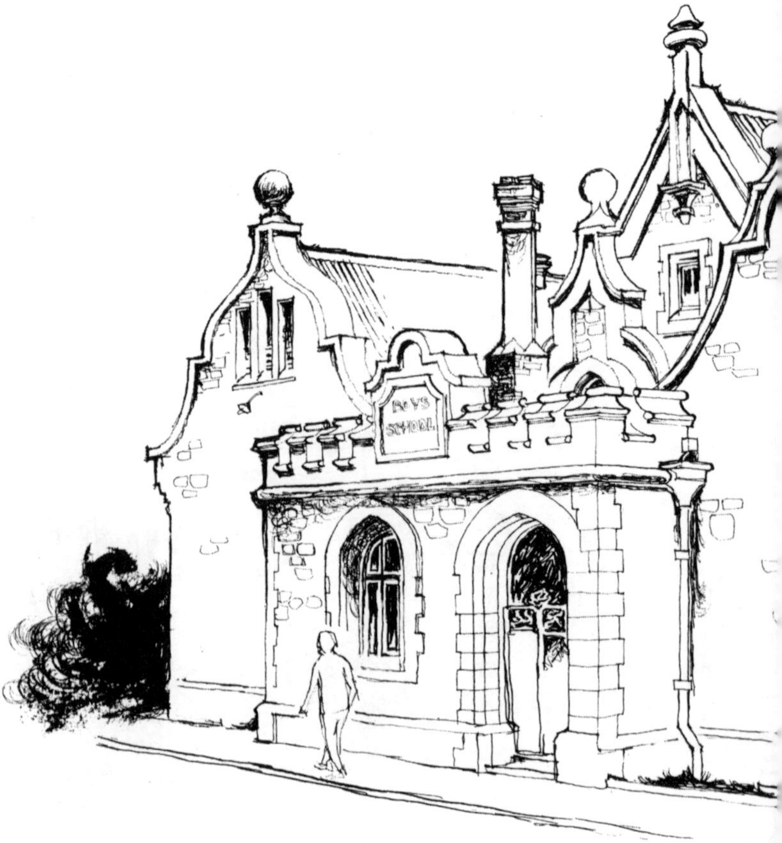

1854, Fremantle Boys' School was built to a design by Colonial Secretary William Sanford, one of a group of extremely talented people involved in early colonial building.

Of all the distinguished citizens who passed through Fremantle Boys' School, probably the most colourful was the man who later became Field-Marshal Sir Thomas Blamey. He was a master at the school for three years at the beginning of the century. It is recorded, in *Fremantle— Preservation and Change*, that Sir Frederick Samson remembers Blamey's cadets drilling in the schoolyard.

This fine relic of colonial days, with its Cape Dutch gables, is to be restored at a cost of around $50,000, and will be used as an institute for the study of film and television.

FREMANTLE GRAMMAR SCHOOL

The existing building—usually known these days as Girton College—was built for the Fremantle Grammar School in 1885. Its founders were the members of St John's Church vestry who, in 1882, saw a need for secondary education in the predominantly Church of England colony. The first Grammar School, which held its classes in a room behind the parsonage, was designed "to give a Christian education to boys of middle-class families," and ultimately it attracted boarders from all parts of the state. It is recorded that by 1891 there were twenty-seven boarders, and ninety-three day scholars.

The founder headmaster was Henry Briggs, who had previously been a teacher at a school in England. He eventually became a prominent figure in Fremantle, and was knighted when he became president of the Legislative Council. Briggs left the Grammar School, however, to found a school of his own. As a consequence the Grammar School, as such, closed. Not long after Briggs' entry into politics, his own school foundered, and the building was taken over by the Misses Haynes for use as a girls' school. This then became Girton College. Although Girton, too, closed in 1930, it is this name which has survived among Fremantle place names.

The crest of the original Grammar School is still to be seen on the south wall of the building.

PROCLAMATION TREE

At the junction of Adelaide and Edward streets, on the fringe of the main central city area of Fremantle, a fine spreading Moreton Bay Fig tree stands defying the traffic of a busy modern intersection. This is the Proclamation Tree,

planted on 21 October 1890—Trafalgar Day—to commemorate the granting of responsible government to the colony of Western Australia.

Governor Sir W. F. Robinson performed the planting ceremony, and the tree was provided by Phillip Webster, an auditor with the Fremantle Council of the day. Forty years later, students of the nearby Fremantle Boys' School donated and mounted a plaque at the site.

Webster, a pioneer tree-lover in an era when reckless tree-felling was the norm, planted many of Fremantle's oldest surviving trees, notably those by St John's Church in Kings Square.

ST PATRICK'S, ADELAIDE STREET

In the earliest years of the colony, the Roman Catholic Church was surprisingly sparsely represented. In *Fremantle —Preservation and Change* it is noted that in 1848 only thirty-seven people, in a population of 503, were Roman Catholics.

However, it is known that from 1843 services were conducted in the Old Court House, on Arthur Head. The first place of worship opened in 1846 in Henry Street. This served the Fremantle congregation until the arrival of the first Sisters of St Joseph in 1855, when a little stone and shingle chapel was built in Adelaide Street. This limestone chapel was replaced in 1900, at a cost of something like $24,000— a vast sum in those days—by the present St Patrick's Church, in Adelaide Street. Then, as now, St Patrick's was probably the most impressive piece of architecture, civic or ecclesiastic, in the whole of Fremantle. It was carried out in fourteenth century Gothic design, and owed its building to the energies of the Reverend Father Tom Ryan, of the Oblate Fathers.

Although the walls of St Patrick's are of local stone, the doorways, turrets, columns, and traceried windows are of Sydney freestone. The magnificent altar is made from imported white marble, and the pews from Western Australian jarrah, which the early settlers called "mahogany." The church is one Fremantle building which seems to be permanently secure against the ambitions of developers. It will assuredly still be serving the large Fremantle Catholic community long after some of its contemporaries, in the architectural sense, have vanished.

WESLEY CHURCH

When the barque *Tranby* arrived at Fremantle in February 1830, one of her 264 passengers was Joseph Hardey, a Wesleyan lay preacher from Yorkshire, who established the Wesley communion in the settlement.

The first services were conducted, according to early diaries, "in the open air under a mahogany tree," but within twelve years a chapel had been built on the site now occupied by the Central Methodist Mission. The chapel, demolished in 1929, served the Wesleyans until the present Wesley Church, in Cantonment Street, was opened in 1888.

The foundation stone of the original chapel was relaid in 1928 and now lies beneath that of the Central Methodist Mission.

Another of Fremantle's interesting old buildings, Scots Church, in South Terrace, was designed by Talbot Hobbs and founded by the Reverend Robert Hamlin. It was built in 1890. To raise funds for the building, churchgoers could reserve seats in the early years for 1s 6d. or 2s 6d.

MUSEUM

"This is the most distinguished group of buildings I have seen in Australia," said Lord Euston, adviser on the preservation of old buildings to the government of the United Kingdom. He spoke in the mid-1960s, and he was looking at what is now Fremantle's Museum and Art Centre in Ord Street.

At that time it stood empty, its windows shattered by vandals, its rooms rank with neglect. The bulldozers seemed to be lurking just round the corner, like hungry monsters straining to be released.

The old place had been, by turns, an asylum for the criminally insane, a home for aged women, and a barracks for United States servicemen during the second World War. Some time in the 1960s it began to attract the attention of what the conservationists call the "knock-the-bloody-thing-down brigade," and for a harrowing period it was in extreme danger of being razed to make way for a public playground.

Its rescuers, who intelligently and aesthetically converted the building to public use, were led by Fremantle's mayor, Sir Frederick Samson.

It now houses, among other things, an interesting and historic maritime museum which displays cannon and relics of the *Batavia*, wrecked off the coast of Western Australia in 1629, and also of the *Gilt Dragon*.

SAMSON HOUSE

The pioneer Samson family has provided Fremantle with three mayors—William Samson 1892–93, Michael Samson 1905–07, and Sir Frederick Samson, who held the mayoral office for twenty-nine years, retiring in 1972.

The original Samson home was at Cliff Street, by the still-enduring warehouse premises. Their next residence, now known simply as the Samson House, is a splendidly-preserved example of colonial domestic architecture. It stands at the corner of Ellen and Ord streets, set in an acre of rose gardens. Sir Frederick Samson, grandson of pioneer Lionel, still sleeps in the old four-poster bed in which he was born. He has lately bequeathed the Samson House as a museum to the Fremantle City Council, together with a collection of period furniture, historic documents, and pictures.

Inside the old home near the kitchen, is an untimbered well seventy feet deep. There is also a still-workable hand-pump, which once supplied water to the camel teams leaving on the long trek to Coolgardie.

RAILWAY STATION

Those whose business in the last century was tied up in river traffic strongly opposed the laying of a railway line from Guildford and Perth to Fremantle, but, of course, the railroad was an inevitable development.

Early opinion was that the line should follow a course south of the river, to Canning Bridge and South Perth, possibly crossing the Swan River to connect with the then Bazaar Terrace jetty. This south-of-the-river plan was devised to avoid obstruction to navigation. However, the line was laid on the north side of the Swan River, and opened on 1 March 1881, when Governor Sir William Robinson travelled down from Perth. The first railway station was opposite Mouat Street, slightly west of today's site.

The present Fremantle Railway Station was opened in July 1907.

Opposite the station, on Phillimore Street, and sited with maximum inconvenience to modern traffic, is an elaborate marble horse-trough and drinking fountain, erected in 1905 by an Englishman named Taylor to the memory of his two sons who died in Western Australia. It seems certain to be moved before long, probably to the nearby park, but Fremantle's preservation-conscious Council is unlikely to allow it to be destroyed.

Railway Station

Though the Cliff Street–Mouat Street section is undoubtedly the "old city," in the early colonial sense, Phillimore Street, running along what used to be the old foreshore, plainly traces the pattern of development eastwards from the Round House area.

The old limestone of the first colony can be seen gradually giving way to brick and tile, to more elaborate and ornate architecture.

Hitchcock, in his *History of Fremantle*, described an area between the buildings on the north side of Phillimore Street and the river shoreline. This was used as a public recreation ground, and was known as The Green. Now there is another pleasant square full of character in the stretch of Phillimore Street between His Majesty's Hotel (on the corner of Mouat Street) and the Custom House at the entrance to Victoria Quay.

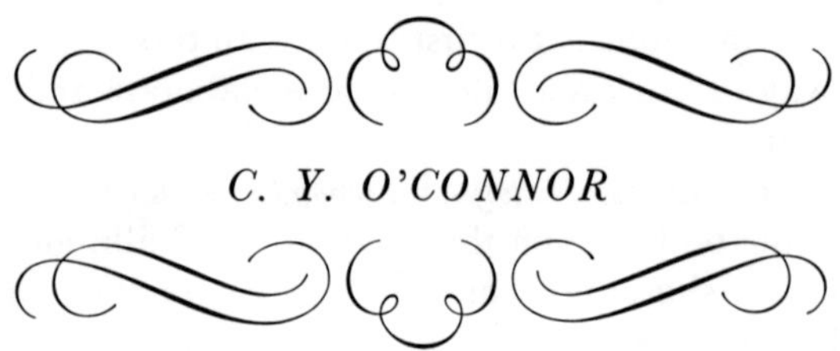

On any given day, when two 45,000-ton liners are discharging at the harbour's 1,350-foot-long passenger terminal at Victoria Quay, one might be forgiven for imagining that the nearby bronze statue of C. Y. O'Connor is laughing quietly.

As engineer-in-chief for Western Australia, the famous O'Connor was so far ahead of his time that all his brilliant plans were widely ridiculed. His plan for an inner harbour was finally adopted in 1891 against a great deal of opposition —some of it at top professional level.

The first load of stone to form the North Mole was tipped in 1892, and the first vessel (s.s. *Sultan* of 2,062 tons from Singapore) entered O'Connor's harbour in 1897.

Today O'Connor's statue is, very probably, one of the first Western Australian sights to be seen by new settlers on their arrival. Behind him the huge Fremantle Port Authority building towers over the entire harbour scene.

GENERAL HARBOUR (1)

Fremantle harbour now handles 10 million tons of cargo each year. Looking at it as it appears today, with its eighteen land-backed berths, its forest of massive cranes, and one of the most modern passenger terminals in Australia, an extraordinary effort of imagination is needed to visualise this river-mouth as it

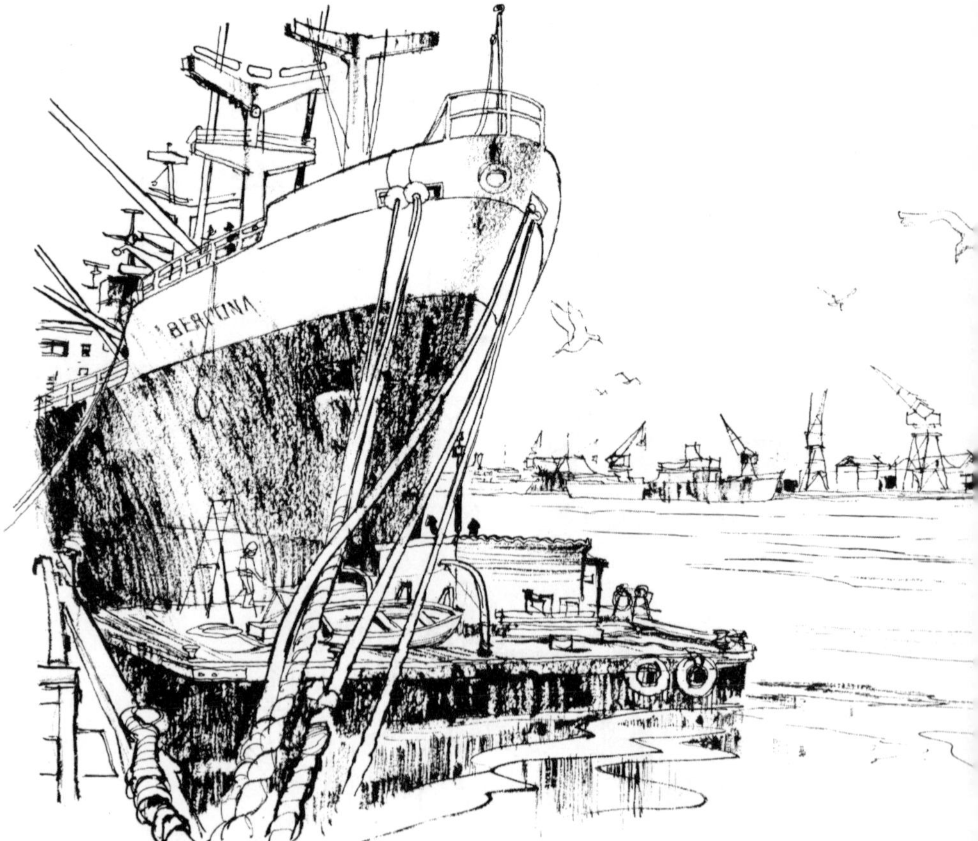

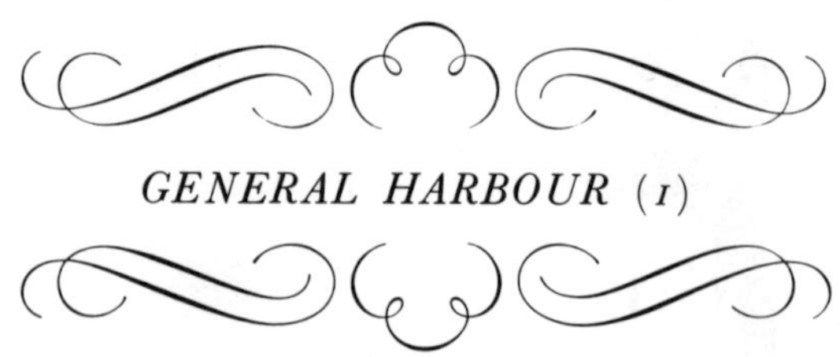

was when the first steamer entered.

The s.s. *Sultan*, with Lady Forrest, wife of Sir John Forrest, at the helm, slipped through the excavated rock bar at the river-mouth on 4 May 1897. The first freighter to use the inner harbour, in October 1897, was the s.s. *Cornwall* from Britain, and the first mail steamer was the German ship s.s. *Gera* in August 1898.

Though bigger and bigger ships followed regularly, it was still exciting to hear, in 1924, that H.M.S. *Hood* (861 feet), and H.M.S. *Repulse* (790 feet) were both berthed, speedily and without trouble, in the inner harbour. Until then there had been lingering doubts that ships of this size could be handled.

With the benefit of hindsight it is easy now to sneer at the misgivings of early colonial engineers who believed that it would be impracticable to open the mouth of the Swan River and to construct therein an inner harbour. But in the nineteenth century the engineering and hydrographic problems involved understandably seemed insuperable to all but the genius C. Y. O'Connor.

Now, breakwaters (North Mole, 4,835 feet long, and South Mole, 2,040 feet long) protect the river-mouth. The channel from Gage Roads to the harbour is dredged to thirty-six feet at low water, and O'Connor's visionary harbour has stretched to 168 acres of protected water, also dredged to thirty-six feet.

Over on the north wharf, Number 1 berth handles bulk petroleum products by pipeline. The great cranes at Number 4 and Number 5 berths unload dry bulk cargo, and Number 9 can bulk-handle grain at up to 1,600 tons an hour.

On top of the Fremantle Port Authority building, watching over it all, is the signal station with a twenty-five-mile range radar-scanner.

FREMANTLE PORT AUTHORITY
STOP

FISHING BOAT HARBOUR

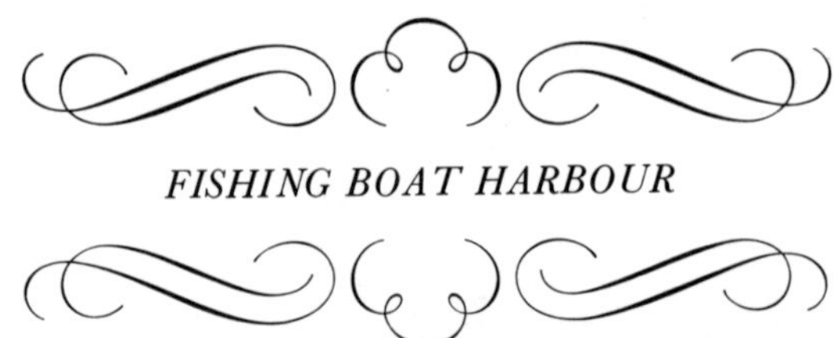

Walk westwards down High Street towards the Round House, turn left along Cliff Street towards the glint of calm water through the Norfolk pines, past the old Government Commissariat Stores, past the quaintly evocative little Croke Lane, past the old Custom House, and you will come

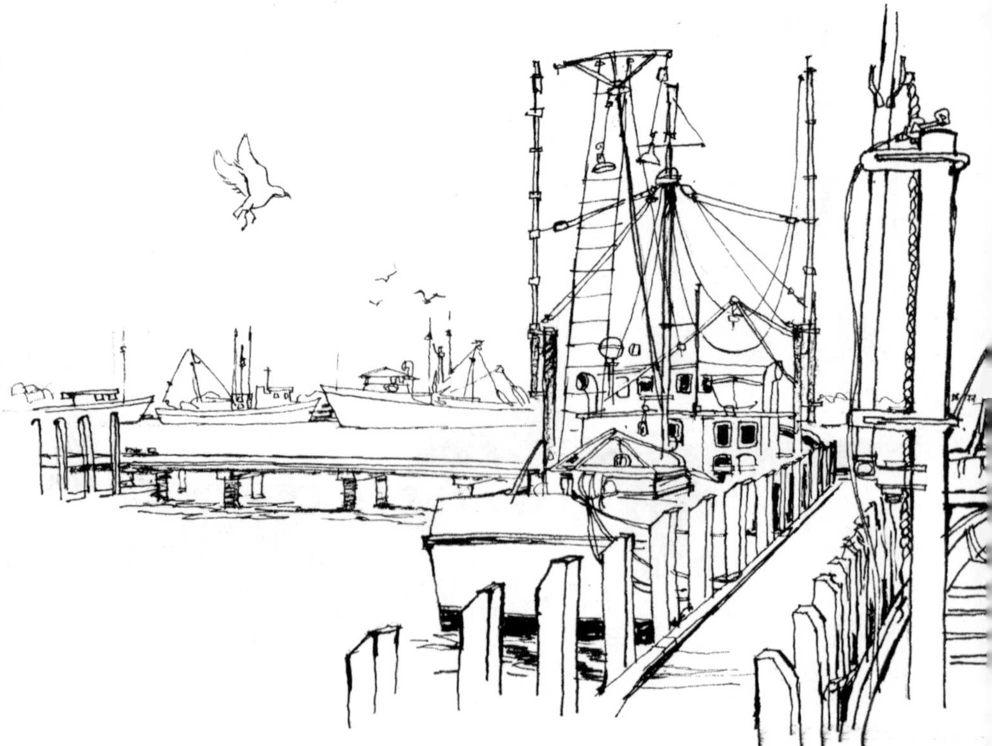

to the Fish Markets. These days you will smell the fragrance of fish-and-chips, and there will probably be piped music, the noise of children at play, and the bustle of shopping centre. Beyond all this, in the small-boat harbour, the fishing fleet jiggles gently on the tide. Fisherman's Wharf, San Francisco, may once have looked like this.

Each year, at the start of the fishing season, a Roman Catholic procession winds its way from St Patrick's Church in Adelaide Street to the little harbour, where the fishing fleet is solemnly blessed. An old bylaw lays down that all fish caught within fifteen miles of Fremantle must be landed at Fish Markets jetty.

FREMANTLE OVAL PAVILION

All manner of oddly-assorted items go towards the overall composition of a city's character. Since no sport, or pastime, has contributed so heavily to the Fremantle scene as Australian Rules Football, it is entirely appropriate to look at the old pavilion at Fremantle Oval.

Originally this area, below the gaol walls, was the parade ground for the pensioners force quartered nearby. It was known then, and for perhaps fifty years afterwards, as Barracks Green Field. It was also used by the Volunteer Defence Force, raised by C. A. Manning in 1861. The brass band of this unit used to draw crowds to the ground.

Deputations from the Fremantle Football and Cricket clubs waited on the council in 1893, asking that the land, then uncommitted to any specific use, be allotted to public recreation. The pavilion, which won a prize for its designer F. W. Burwell, was opened by Sir John Forrest on 6 November 1897.

In the casually tasteless way of the times, the historical and picturesque name of Barracks Green Field was dropped in favour of the mundane Fremantle Oval.

A point of more modern interest is that the galvanised steel goalposts at Fremantle Oval (now the home ground of the South Fremantle Football Club) are at thirty-two feet the tallest in Western Australia, and are exactly the same height as those used at the Melbourne Cricket Ground. The posts taper from a four-inch base to a three-inch top, causing many people to imagine, incorrectly, that they lean inwards.

PHONE
HERE

WAR MEMORIALS

Fremantle's memorial to the dead of the first World War was the result of public subscription in 1927. It was erected on Monument Hill, and unveiled on Anzac Day 1928.

A history of Fremantle, written by Dr J. S. Battye, then Chief State Librarian, was placed in a capsule in the foundations. It was hoped then—though it is not so today—that "the first Australian object that will meet the eyes of travellers coming from the westward" would naturally be this memorial on the highest hill in the district.

After the second World War, additions were made to the original memorial. Later still, a torpedo presented by the United States Navy was mounted nearby to commemorate U.S.N. personnel who died on active service while based at Fremantle.

On Trafalgar Day (21 October) 1972 the thirty-foot periscope from H.M. Submarine *Tabbard* was added to the memorials on Monument Hill, in memory of British and Allied submariners who gave their lives while operating from Fremantle during the second World War.

FREMANTLE
THE HARBO
C.Y. O'Connor
Railway Station
MARKET
FPA Building
PHILLIMORE
ST
PAKENHAM
ST
Cleo Hotel
HIGH
ST
HENRY ST
MOUAT ST
Round House
Samson Bldg
CLIFF ST
Court House
Govt. Stores
Old Custom House
MARINE TCE
Esplanade
Fishing Boat Harbour

ACKNOWLEDGMENTS

I am particularly grateful to Mr Murray Edmonds, of the Fremantle City Council, for his help in compiling this book. My thanks, also to Sir Frederick Samson and Mrs Laurie; Mr Laurie Strutt, P.R.O., P.M.G. Department; Mr Ted Joll of West Australian Newspapers Ltd; Mr John Birch, Fremantle City Council Librarian; and Mr Murray Rann, Fremantle Port Authority.

Reference books which have greatly simplified research are: *History of Fremantle* by J. K. Hitchcock; *Fremantle—Preservation and Change* by Fremantle City Council; *Cyclopedia of Western Australia* by Dr J. S. Battye; *Western Gateway: A History of Fremantle* by J. K. Ewers; *The Port of Fremantle* (*First in Australia*) issued by Fremantle Port Authority; and *Gateway*, a journal issued by the City of Fremantle.